DESERT ANIMALS Searchin' for Shade

Camel

by Meish Goldish

Consultant:

Anne Innis Dagg, PhD
Independent Studies
University of Waterloo
Waterloo, Ontario, Canada

BEARPORT PUBLISHING

New York, New York

Credits

Cover, © Yasser El Dershaby/Shutterstock, Ivan Pavlov/Shutterstock, and Lenar Musin/Shutterstock; TOC, © ekipaj/Shutterstock; 4–5, © Ivan Pavlov/Shutterstock; 7, © eAlisa/Shutterstock; 7B, © Aleksandr Hunta/Shutterstock; 8, © Wolfgang Zwanger/Shutterstock; 9, © Paul Prescott/Shutterstock; 10T, © murengstockphoto/Shutterstock; 10B, © Erez Herrnstadt/Alamy; 11, © Laszlo Halasi/Shutterstock; 12, © Craig Lovell/Corbis; 13, © Erni/Shutterstock; 14, © LOOK Die Bildagentur der Fotografen GmbH/Alamy; 15, © Frans Lemmens/Alamy; 16–17, © John Carnemolla/Thinkstock; 18, © Simon Snozyk/age fotostock; 19, © Hanne & Jens Eriksen/naturepl.com; 20, © gnomeandi/Shutterstock; 21, © Stockfolio®/Alamy; 21BL, © age fotostock Spain, SL/Alamy; 22TL, © gnomeandi/Shutterstock; 22TR, © Fatseyeva/Shutterstock; 22ML, © Berit Kessler/Shutterstock; 22MR, © Guenter Guni/Thinkstock; 22BL, © eAlisa/Shutterstock; 22BR, © Laszlo Halasi/Shutterstock; 23TL, © Craig Burrows/Shutterstock; 23TM, © eAlisa/Shutterstock; 23TR, © Ivan Pavlov/Shutterstock; 23BL, © Paul Vinten/Shutterstock; 23BM, © Anze Bizjan/Shutterstock; 23BR, © Aleksandr Hunta/Shutterstock.

Publisher: Kenn Goin
Creative Director: Spencer Brinker
Editor: Jessica Rudolph
Design: Alix Wood

Library of Congress Cataloging-in-Publication Data

Goldish, Meish.
  Camel / by Meish Goldish.
      pages cm.—(Desert animals : searchin' for shade)
  Includes bibliographical references and index.
  ISBN 978-1-62724-536-4 (library binding)—ISBN 1-62724-536-7 (library binding)
  1. Camels—Juvenile literature. I. Title.
  QL737.U54G65 2015
  599.63'62—dc23
                    2014037365

For more information, write to Bearport Publishing Company, Inc., 45 West 21st Street, Suite 3B, New York, New York 10010. Printed in the United States of America.

10 9 8 7 6 5 4 3 2 1

Contents

Taking the Heat

It's a summer day in the **desert**.

A tall animal with a **hump** on its back walks slowly across the hot sand.

It's a camel looking for plants to eat.

The animal hasn't had a drink of water in a week—but it's not thirsty.

The camel is very comfortable in its hot, dry home!

In deserts where camels live, temperatures can rise to more than 120°F (49°C) and drop to below freezing.

hump

How would you describe a camel to someone who has never seen one?

One Hump or Two?

Most camels have one hump.

They are called **dromedary,** or Arabian, camels.

The other kind of camel—the **Bactrian**—has two humps.

Dromedaries live in deserts throughout Asia, Africa, and Australia.

Bactrian camels live only in a few desert areas in Asia.

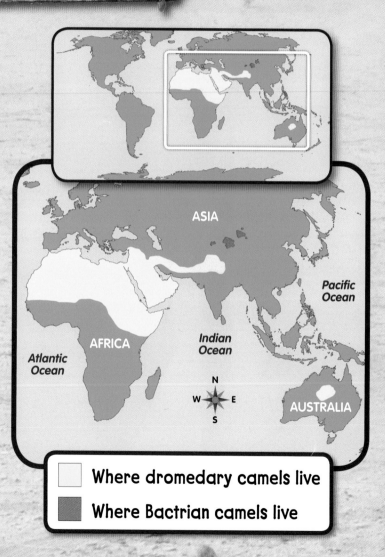

ASIA

Pacific Ocean

AFRICA

Indian Ocean

Atlantic Ocean

AUSTRALIA

☐ Where dromedary camels live

■ Where Bactrian camels live

Dromedaries are big—more than 7 feet (2 m) tall at the hump. They can weigh up to 1,600 pounds (726 kg). That's about as heavy as a large horse.

Why do you think camels have humps?

dromedary camel

Bactrian camel

Fantastic Fat

A camel's hump helps it survive in its dry desert home. How?

The hump holds up to 80 pounds (36 kg) of fat.

The camel lives on the fat when there is no food or water around.

The fat gives the camel energy and keeps its body from getting dry in the hot desert.

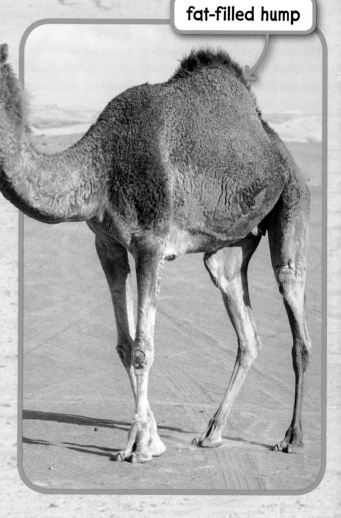

fat-filled hump

A camel can go for about two weeks without drinking water. When it does find water to drink, it can swallow 35 gallons (132 l) in 10 minutes. That's like drinking 560 glasses of water at one time!

Besides its hump, what other parts of a camel do you think help it survive in the desert?

Sand Walker

A camel can move easily across the desert sand, thanks to its large, flat feet.

Thick pads cover the bottoms of the animal's feet.

Every time the camel takes a step, the pads spread.

This keeps the camel's feet from sinking into the soft sand.

The pads also protect the animal as it walks on hot sand and bumpy rocks.

camel's foot

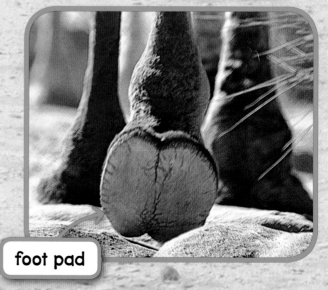

foot pad

A camel's knees have thick skin called calluses. The calluses allow the camel to rest on the hot sand without feeling pain.

How do you think a camel's nose, eyelashes, and ears help the animal survive in the desert?

11

Sand Everywhere!

When the wind blows hard in the desert, grains of sand swirl everywhere.

A camel's eyelashes, ears, and nose help protect the animal.

Two rows of long, curly eyelashes keep sand from blowing into its eyes.

Fur inside its ears also keeps out sand.

The camel can even close its **nostrils** to keep from breathing in tiny grains of sand.

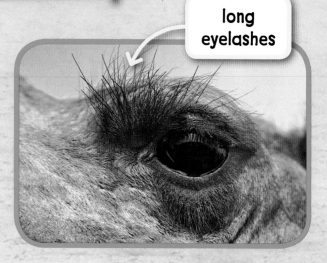

long eyelashes

Most animals have two eyelids over each eye, but camels have three. The third eyelid, which is see-through, clears sand away from the eyeball.

13

Plant Menu

The camel is a plant-eater.

It eats almost any plant it can find, such as grasses and saltbushes.

Many plants that a camel eats contain water.

As a result, the camel doesn't have to spend too much time searching for water to drink.

The animal gets some of the water it needs to survive from the plants.

grass

Camels have thick, tough lips. They help the animals eat the prickly thorns that grow on some plants.

Starting a Family

Camels don't live in the desert alone.

Instead, they live in groups.

One group, which can have up to 20 camels, includes several adults and their young.

In winter, male and female camels from the same group **mate**.

About 14 months later, the female gives birth to a baby called a calf.

The female camel finds a private spot to give birth. She and her calf will go back to the group about two weeks later.

mother

calf

How soon after they are born do you think baby camels start to walk?

A baby calf quickly learns how to keep up with its group.

Thirty minutes after it is born, the calf can already walk.

A few hours later, it can run, too!

For 12 to 18 months, the baby drinks its mother's milk.

At around four years old, the young camel is an adult member of its group.

a newborn calf running

A newborn calf weighs around 80 pounds (36 kg). Usually, a female camel gives birth to only one calf, but sometimes she has two.

a calf drinking milk
from its mother

Ships of the Desert

Camels are known as "ships of the desert." Why?

Many people who live in the desert ride camels or use them to carry goods.

One adult camel can carry nearly 500 pounds (227 kg) of goods.

People also drink camel's milk and make cheese and butter with the milk.

They use camel hair to make clothing.

Camels help people survive in the hot, dry desert!

a rider on a camel

Camels can live about 40 years.

camel's milk

Science Lab

Be a Camel Scientist

Imagine you are a scientist who studies dromedary camels.

Look at each of these pictures and see if you can figure out what the camel is doing.

Then use the pictures to tell your friends and family what you've learned about dromedary camels.

(The answers are on page 24.)

1

2

3

4

5

6

Science Words

Bactrian (BAK-tree-uhn) a camel with two humps

desert (DEZ-urt) dry land with little rainfall and few plants; some deserts are covered with sand

dromedary (DROM-uh-dair-ee) a camel with one hump; also called an Arabian camel

hump (HUHMP) a large lump that sticks up from a camel's back, where fat is stored

mate (MAYT) to come together in order to have young

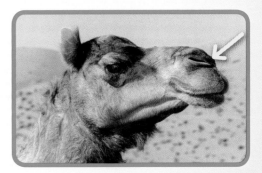

nostrils (NOSS-truhlz) openings in the nose that are used for breathing and smelling

Index

Read More

Borgert-Spaniol, Megan. *Camels (Blastoff! Readers: Animal Safari).* Minneapolis, MN: Bellwether Media (2012).

Gish, Melissa. *Camels (Living Wild).* Mankato, MN: Creative Education (2013).

Riggs, Kate. *Camels (Amazing Animals).* Mankato, MN: Creative Education (2014).

Learn More Online

To learn more about camels, visit **www.bearportpublishing.com/DesertAnimals**

About the Author

Meish Goldish has written more than 200 books for children. His book *Surf Dog Miracles* was a Children's Choices Selection in 2014. He lives in Brooklyn, New York, and enjoys visiting the camels at the Bronx Zoo.

Answers for Page 22

1. carrying a person
2. eating a desert plant
3. a baby drinking its mother's milk
4. drinking water
5. carrying goods
6. resting on the hot sand